The Jews

Casey Horton

CRABTREE
Publishing Company

CRABTREE
Publishing Company

PMB 16A, 350 Fifth Avenue
Suite 3308
New York, NY 10118

612 Welland Avenue
St. Catharines, Ontario
Canada L2M 5V6

Co-ordinating editor: Ellen Rodger
Content editor: Virginia Mainprize
Production co-ordinator: Rosie Gowsell
Cover design: Robert MacGregor

Film: Embassy Graphics
Printer: Worzalla Publishing Company

Created by:
Brown Partworks Ltd
Commissioning editor: Anne O'Daly
Project editor: Caroline Beattie
Picture researcher: Adrian Bentley
Editorial assistant: Chris Wiegand
Maps: Mark Walker
Consultant: Donald Avery, Ph.D.

CATALOGING-IN-PUBLICATION DATA
Horton, Casey.
    The Jews / Casey Horton.
        p.cm.– (We Came to North America)
    Includes index.
    Summary: Descriptive test and eyewitness accounts
describe how Jews from around the world fled persecution
in their homelands and came to North America.
    ISBN 0-7787-0187-5 – ISBN 0-7787-0201-4 (pbk.)
        1. Jews–United States–History–Juvenile literature. 2. Jews-
-Canada–History–Juvenile literature. 3. Immigrants–United
States–Juvenile literature. 4. Immigrants–Canada–Juvenile
literature. [1. Jews–United States-History. 2. Jews–Canada–
History. 3. United States– Emigration and immigration. 4.
Canada–Emigration and immigration.] I. Title. II. Series.
    E184.35.H67 2000
    973'.04924–dc21   LC 00-020635
                                                  CIP

Photographs:
AKG London 7 (bottom), 21(bottom); Erich
Lessing 8; The Art Archive, 13 (bottom); British
Library 6 (bottom); Ashkenaz Foundation,
Toronto (Ashkenaz Festival Poster: Original
papercut by Barbara Klunder. Design and digital
imaging by Louis Fishauf/Reactor) 25 (top);
Brown Partworks Library of Congress 13 (top),
15; Corbis 17 (top); Bettmann 20 (bottom);
Bojan Brecelj 25 (bottom); David H. Wells 5
(top); Dean Conger 6 (top); Kelly-Mooney
Photography 4 (bottom); Mitchell Gerber 30
(bottom); Museum of the City of New York
21(top); Richard T. Nowitz 29 (bottom right);
Ted Spiegel 28; The Purcell Team 30 (top); Wally
McNamee 31(bottom); Hulton Getty 9, 11, 19,
24, 27 (bottom), 31(top); The Image Bank
Archive Photos front cover, 7(top), 16, 17
(bottom), 29 (left); Mark Azavedo 29 (top right);
North Wind Picture Archives 5 (bottom), 20
(top); Peter Newark's Pictures 4 (top), 12, 23, 26
(top) back cover; Robert Hunt Library 26
(bottom), 27 (top).

Cover: A modern-day klezmer band. This
lively music dates back over 500 years and
is still popular today.

Book credits
Page 10: *The Promised Land* by Mary
Antin, Penguin 20th Century Classics, 1997.
Page 14: *Ellis Island: Echoes from a
Nation's Past*, Susan Jonas ed., published
by Aperture, in association with the
National Park Service, U.S. Department of
the Interior, and Montclair State College.
Page 18: *How the Other Half Lives* by
Jacob Riis, Charles Scribner's Sons, 1901.
Page 22: *Destination America* by Maldwyn
A. Jones, Holt, Rinehart & Winston, 1976.

Contents

Introduction

◀ Immigrants usually move into the same district when they arrive in their new country. This picture shows the Polish Jewish area of Chicago in the early twentieth century.

The Jewish people who settled in North America between the seventeenth and twentieth centuries came in search of a land of hope and freedom. Some came seeking better business opportunities. Some came to find a place where they could freely practice their traditions and religion. Many were fleeing great hardship and cruelty. All were hoping to build a new life for themselves and their families.

The first Jewish **immigrants** came to North America in 1654. They were Spanish Jews, searching for a new home where they would be treated equally and would be free to practice their religion. Over the next three centuries, four waves of Jewish immigrants followed. The first was the arrival of more Spanish Jews, known as Sephardim. Many settled in South Carolina, where Charleston had the largest Jewish population. In 1776, at the time of the American Revolution, there were 2000 Jews living in the United States. They were accepted as equals by the other **colonists**. Later, until the mid-1800s, most Jews coming to Canada and the United States were from Germany. Many had been successful business people in Europe, and they **prospered** in their new countries.

▼ A Jewish man leads school children off a school bus in Montréal.

Who Are the Jews?

Today's Jews have come from many different parts of the world, belong to many different **races**, and live in many countries. The word "Jew" has come to describe those who follow the religion known as Judaism. However, there are people who think of themselves as Jewish and have Jewish parents, but who no longer practice Judaism.

Most Jews are the **descendants** of people who trace their **ancestry** back 4000 years to a shepherd called Abraham. According to the Bible, Abraham left his home, in what is today Iraq, and traveled west with his family and his sheep. In Canaan, he founded a tribe of people called the Hebrews. Unlike other tribes, who worshiped many gods, the Hebrews worshiped only one God.

▲ **Two Orthodox students discuss a point of Jewish law.**

The largest wave of Jewish immigration was between 1880 and the early 1900s. Russian and Polish Jews came in huge numbers, fleeing from **persecution**. They believed that North America would be a place of unlimited opportunity. Most landed and settled in New York City. However, Jewish communities sprang up in other U.S. and Canadian centers.

These immigrants arrived with no money, and many could not read or write. They had to take any job they could find. A few quickly became wealthy and successful. Most Jews who came during this time, however, lived and worked in dreadful conditions, struggling to give their children a good education and a better future. They believed that education was the key to success. Their children studied hard and became successful doctors, teachers, lawyers, scientists, and business people.

After World War II, a smaller group of Jewish immigrants came to find a new home in North America. They were escaping from war-torn Europe. They were the **survivors** of the Holocaust, the mass murder of Jews by German Nazis. These millions of Jewish immigrants built new lives for themselves and their families in their adopted countries. At times, even in North America, they suffered from unequal and unfair treatment. Today, they are respected citizens, whose contributions to the arts, business, the **professions**, and science are widely recognized.

▲ **In immigrant families, even the children had to work. These boys sold home-made pretzels.**

A Long History

For almost two thousand years, Jews had no homeland. Often and in many places, they were treated unequally or even attacked and murdered.

▲ This Torah, a scroll on which the first five books of the Bible are written, is thought to be the oldest in the world.

Most Jews today, whether they live in North America or the rest of the world, are the descendants of the ancient Hebrews. Thousands of years ago, in biblical times, they lived in the land that is now called Israel. About two thousand years ago, their country was conquered by the Romans. The Jews fled and settled in Europe, the Middle East, and as far away as India. They formed communities that became centers of Jewish learning. This scattering of the Jews in lands far away from their homeland is called the Diaspora.

Wherever they went, Jews were a **minority** group. Sometimes, they were welcomed, as in Spain when it was controlled by the **Muslims**. At other times, they were **discriminated** against, especially by **Christians** in Europe. This hatred and persecution of the Jews is known as anti-Semitism.

Jews were tolerated and even accepted when times were good. However, when times were bad or there were wars, the Jews were blamed and often persecuted. They were forced to live in walled-off parts of cities and towns, called ghettos. They had to wear a badge or special clothing that showed they were Jews. They were not allowed to work at most jobs or to own land.

▶ A beautifully decorated page from a Spanish Torah. The writing is in Hebrew.

Arrival in New Amsterdam

In September 1654, 23 Jewish people arrived in New York City, which was then called New Amsterdam. They had originally fled from persecution in Spain. Their arrival marks the beginning of Jewish settlement in North America. Within the next 100 years, other Jewish communities were established in Savannah, Philadelphia, Newport, and Charleston. Jews had the same rights as everyone else in the American colonies. They built their own synagogues, or temples, and could practice their religion freely. They worked hard and became successful business people.

▲ **A synagogue in Newport, Rhode Island, in the early 1700s.**

About 600 years ago, all the Jews from England and France were **expelled**. Thousands fled to Poland, which encouraged them to come because of their many talents.

In 1492, after the Christians had defeated the Muslims in Spain, Jews were forced to leave that country. However, some stayed and pretended to become Christians. These Jews continued to practice their Jewish faith in secret.

Through all these troubles, the Jews survived. They kept up their **culture**, religion, and traditions, often in secret. In the late 1700s, attitudes toward the Jews began to improve in Europe. Many people began to demand equal rights for all people, including Jews. In many Western European countries, Jews were given the same rights as other people. They were allowed to go to university. They could enter professions which they had not been allowed to take up in the past. Some Jews became famous musicians, writers, scientists, and doctors.

▶ **In 1614, in Frankfurt, Germany, Christians stole and destroyed Jewish property.**

Flight from Terror

In the late nineteenth century, when life for Jews was improving in most parts of Europe, conditions were getting worse in Russia. Since the rule of Catherine the Great (1752–1796), Jews had been persecuted in that country.

▲ The Jewish Quarter in Cracow, Poland, in the nineteenth century.

Poland, the home of the largest number of Jews in Europe, was divided in 1795. A large part of the country was given to Russia, and Polish Jews found themselves under Russian rule. By the end of the nineteenth century, over five million Jews were living in that country.

Russia had often been **intolerant** of people of other religions. In 1792, Catherine the Great forced most Russian Jews to live in a part of the country called the Pale. Jews had to live in towns or cities and could not own land. They were heavily taxed and were forbidden to work at many jobs. Boys, as young as twelve years old, were taken from their families and forced to join the army where they had to stay for 30 years. Jewish girls were not allowed to go to school.

The Pale of Settlement

Most of the Jews who came to North America at the end of the nineteenth century were from the Pale. This area in southwestern Russia was set up in the 1790s to prevent Jews from living in the capital or any other of the Russian provinces. Strict laws forbade Jews from owning land. Most were moneylenders, artisans, or merchants trading with Russian peasants who worked as farmers. Taxes on Jews were so high that most lived in terrible poverty.

▶ **In Russia, the Jews lived within the Pale.**

In 1881, when the Russian **czar** Alexander II was **assassinated**, the government encouraged Russian Christians to take out their anger on Jews. A violent wave of anti-Semitism hit the country. New laws made life for Jews unbearable. The area of the Pale was cut down, and Jews had to stay inside the Jewish area of their town, known as the ghetto. Jewish merchants, now forbidden to trade with non-Jews, could no longer support themselves and their families. Many lived in such poverty that they became sick or starved. In attacks against Jews, called pogroms, hundreds of Jews were **massacred** and their homes were destroyed. One hundred thousand Jews were left homeless in one year alone. The bloodshed continued for more than ten years.

Between 1881 and 1900, more than a million Jews left Russia to escape the horror. Many traveled to Canada and the United States to seek a new life free from persecution.

◀ **During this pogrom, in Russia, Jews were imprisoned in an arsenal, a place where arms and ammunition are stored.**

Eyewitness to History

Pogroms, during which Jews across Russia were beaten and murdered, and Jewish homes were burned, continued into the early twentieth century. MARY ANTIN, who emigrated from Russia to Boston, wrote the following description of what it was like to be Jewish in a country where Jews were persecuted.

" I remember a time when I thought a pogrom had broken out in our street, and I wonder that I did not die of fear. It was some Christian holiday, and we had been warned by the police to keep indoors. Gates were locked; shutters were barred... Fearful and yet curious, we looked through the cracks in the shutters. We saw a procession of peasants and townspeople, led by a number of priests, carrying crosses and banners and images.... The streets were considered too holy for Jews to be about; and we lived in fear till the end of the day, knowing that the least disturbance might start a riot, and a riot lead to a pogrom. "

The Journey

The journey from Europe to North America was long and sometimes terrifying. Right up to the end of the nineteenth century, Jews who left their homes full of hope faced many difficulties before they reached their destination.

Until the 1880s, Jewish **emigrants** traveling to North America crossed the Atlantic in sailing ships. The journey took up to three months and cost a family all its life's savings. Often the father came first and sent for his family after he had found work and saved enough money.

▲ Jewish immigrants left everything behind, bringing only what they could carry.

Jews had to travel long distances from Russia to the ports from which their ships sailed. They began their journey by making their way from their home to a railroad station in a city such as Kiev or Warsaw. A train took them to a large city in central Europe, such as Vienna, Berlin, and Breslau. From there, many traveled by train to the ports of Hamburg or Bremen, where they boarded their ship for North America. Others traveled first to England, landing at Harwich, Grimsby, or London. They then made their way to the port of Liverpool to sail to New York, Montréal, and Québec City. Most crossings were made between March and October, to avoid winter. Even then the sea was very rough. Many passengers suffered from weeks of seasickness.

▶ To travel to North America, many Jews first had to make a long train journey across Europe.

Landing in New York

The early immigrants landing in New York **disembarked** at Castle Garden, and later, between 1892 and 1942, at Ellis Island. When the exhausted immigrants arrived, they still had to go through a physical and mental examination to see if they were fit to enter the country. They were herded into a huge hall, examined by doctors for signs of sickness and disease and questioned by immigration officers. Some, who could not pass all the exams, were sent back to Europe. For many immigrants, Ellis Island was known as Heartbreak Island.

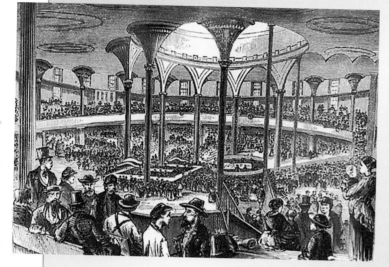

◄ **Hundreds of immigrants arriving in Castle Garden in 1871.**

On board ship, Jewish immigrants were packed together, along with other immigrants, in the "steerage" of the ship — the cheapest area. Here, under the deck, they had to do everything: eat and sleep, and meet all their other needs, including washing and toileting. They spent most of the voyage lying in narrow bunks. Overcrowding led to outbreaks of disease: typhus, smallpox, and cholera. The conditions were so dreadful that, in the United States, the Senate investigated the situation in 1854. One government official reported that even cattle crossing the ocean traveled under better conditions than these poor Jewish immigrants. However, little was done at that time to improve matters and many people died during the crossing. By 1881, most of the sailing ships had been replaced by much faster steamships.

► **Two Jewish men wait up on deck as their ship pulls into New York harbor.**

Eyewitness to History

ARNOLD WEISS came from Russia and arrived at Ellis Island with his family in 1921, at the age of thirteen.

" They also questioned people on **literacy**. My uncle called me aside, when he came to take us off. He said, 'Your mother doesn't know how to read.' I said, 'That's all right.' For the reading you faced what they called the commissioners, like judges on a bench. I was surrounded by my aunt and uncle and another uncle who's a pharmacist – my mother was in the center. They said she would have to take a test of reading. Some man said, 'She can't speak English.' Another man said, 'We know that. We will give her a siddur.' You know what a siddur is? It's a Jewish book. The night they said this, I knew that she couldn't do that and we would be in trouble.

Well, they opened up a siddur. There was a certain passage they had you read. I looked at it and I saw right away what it was. I quickly studied it – I knew the whole paragraph. Then I got underneath the two of them there – I was very small – and I told her the words in Yiddish very softly. I had memorized the lines and I said them quietly and she said them louder so the commissioner could hear it. She looked at it and it sounded as if she was reading it, but I was doing the talking underneath. "

THE AMERICANESE WALL, AS CONGRESSMAN
BURNETT WOULD BUILD IT.
Uncle Sam: You're welcome in — if you can climb it!

A New Home

In 1851, there were 50,000 Jews living in the United States. Thirty years later, the Jewish population had grown to 250,000. By 1929, two and a half million more Jews had landed in the U.S. and Canada. They were Russian-Polish Jews who had left home, seeking a new life.

Almost 65 per cent of all the Russian and Polish immigrants to North America landed and stayed in New York City. The city was growing quickly, and there was a need for cheap labor. Like other immigrants at the time, Jews moved to the neighborhoods where people of the same **nationality** lived. In New York, they settled in the Hebrew section, in overcrowded **tenements**.

Jews, along with millions of other immigrants, settled in the poorest and most run-down districts. Large families of ten or more people lived in dark, cramped, two-room apartments. Sometimes, they were so poor that they had to take in boarders. Six or more people slept in a single room, and four children were crammed into the same bed. Usually, the toilet was down the hall and was shared with other families in the building. Water came from a **communal** tap. Tenements were hot in the summer and cold and damp in the winter.

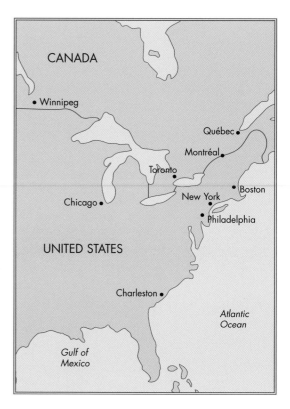

▲ After their long journey across the Atlantic, most Jews settled in the east, though some traveled west to Winnipeg in Canada and Chicago in the United States.

◄ This man lived in a coal cellar. This 1895 photo, shows him preparing for Sabbath, the Jewish holy day.

Help for the Needy

As more and more immigrants arrived in North America, Jewish charities were formed to help those in need: the poor, the orphans, the hungry, the sick, the dying, and the **bereaved**. The first organization was the Hebrew Benevolent Society, formed in 1824. In 1843, Henry Jones founded the order of B'nai B'rith (Hebrew for "Sons of the Covenant"), now the oldest and largest Jewish aid organization in the world. The American Jewish Congress, set up in 1918, and the Canadian Jewish Congress, founded in 1919, worked to promote Jewish rights.

▲ **North American Jews helped each other by giving food parcels to those in need.**

Most of the new immigrants had little or no money when they arrived in North America. They had spent their savings on the long journey, and they desperately needed to find work. In their homeland, where Jews were limited in the jobs they were allowed to do, many had worked as tailors and seamstresses. In Canada and the United States where the garment industry was booming, there was a demand for people with needlework skills, and many new Jewish immigrants found work in the garment industry.

Many Jewish immigrants had been traders or **peddlers** in their towns and villages in Russia, buying and selling old clothes and secondhand goods. When they arrived in America, they often continued this work, going from door to door collecting and selling scrap and old rags. After years of hauling heavy packs on their backs, they saved enough money to buy a horse and cart. As their businesses grew, some of these immigrants opened stores and became wealthy and successful **entrepeneurs**.

▼ **This photograph, taken in 1872, shows a row of tenement houses in New York City.**

Eyewitness to History

The writer of the following piece, JACOB A. RIIS (1849–1914), describes what life was like in the Hebrew Quarter of New York in the last half of the nineteenth century.

"It is said that nowhere in the world are so many people crowded together in a square mile as here. The average five-story tenement adds a story or two to its stature in Ludlow Street and an extra building on the rear lot, and yet the sign "To Let" is the rarest of all there. Here is one seven stories high. The sanitary policeman whose beat it is will tell you that it contains thirty-six families. In this house, where a case of smallpox was reported, there were 58 babies, and 38 children that were over the age of five. In Essex Street two small rooms in a six-story tenement were made to hold a 'family' of father and mother, twelve children, and six boarders.

The homes of the Hebrew quarter are its workshop also. You are made fully aware of it before you have traveled the length of a single block in any of these East Side streets, by the whir of one thousand sewing machines, worked at high pressure from earliest dawn till mind and muscle give out together. Every member of the family, from the youngest to the oldest, bears a hand, shut in the qualmy rooms, where meals are cooked and clothing washed and dried besides, the livelong day. It is not unusual to find a dozen persons – many women and children – at work in a single small room."

Sweatshop Work

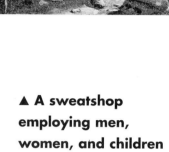

By 1914, New York City was home to more than 450,000 Jewish immigrants. Many of these people, and many Jews in other large cities, worked in sweatshops.

Sweatshop was the name given to places where people, mostly new immigrants, worked long hours for low pay, in terrible conditions. Many of the workers made clothes for the garment industry. The population of North America was growing rapidly, and there was a huge demand for clothes.

Sweatshop owners were paid for each piece of clothing they sold. Because they wanted as high a profit as possible, they paid their workers as little as they could. Sometimes, they used their own homes as sweatshops and crammed in as many workers as possible.

▲ A sweatshop employing men, women, and children in the 1890s.

▼ The whole family in this pantmaker's workshop earned $8 per week.

Fire!

In 1909, workers in the clothing industry went on strike to demand better conditions in sweatshops and factories. Although the strikers were successful, conditions did not improve soon enough to prevent a terrible tragedy.

In 1911, fire broke out in the Triangle Waist Company in New York, a clothing factory in which the workers were mainly women. Some were as young as fifteen years old. The fire broke out on a Saturday afternoon, when hundreds

▲ **The firefighters arrived too late to save 146 workers in the fire at the Triangle Waist Company.**

of workers were in the building. Although city inspectors had classed it as safe, the building only had one fire escape. Many workers were saved by climbing across the roof, but 146 people died. After this tragedy, the authorities set up a Factory Investigating Commission. One of its aims was to reduce the danger of fire in factories.

In good weather, some workers were put on the balcony, the roof, or the fire escape. Workers were at their sewing machines from early morning until late at night – often from 5 am to 9 pm, and even until 2 or 3 am when times were busy. Often they were so tired that they did not go home at night and slept over their machines.

▼ **These women belonged to the Women's Trade Union League. They went on strike for better working conditions.**

Sweatshops were unhealthy, dirty, sunless, and without air. They were filled with constant noise of machinery. Men were paid around $7 a week, and women $3-$6. Eventually, workers got together to demand better and safer working conditions and more money. They formed organizations called trade unions. In the garment industry, many of the members and the leaders of the trade unions were Jewish.

Eyewitness to History

Immigrant children often started work at about eight or nine years old to help support their families. By 1900, 26 U.S. states had laws controlling child labor, including setting an age at which children could start working. However, these laws usually only applied to children under fourteen, and they were not strictly enforced. Many working children were under age. In the following account, PAULINE NEWMAN, who immigrated with her family to New York in 1907, describes how she went to work in a factory producing shirtwaists, which were women's blouses and dresses with details copied from men's shirts.

“ It was child's work, since we were all children. We had a corner in the factory which was like a kindergarten. The work wasn't difficult. The shirtwaist finished by the operator would come to us so we could cut off the thread left by the needle of the machine. You had little scissors because you were children. Somehow the boss knew when the inspector was coming. Materials came in high wooden cases and when the inspector came we were put in them and covered with shirtwaists. By the time he arrived there were no children.

In the busy season we worked seven days a week. That's why the sign went up on the freight elevator: 'If you don't come in on Sunday, don't come in on Monday.' ”

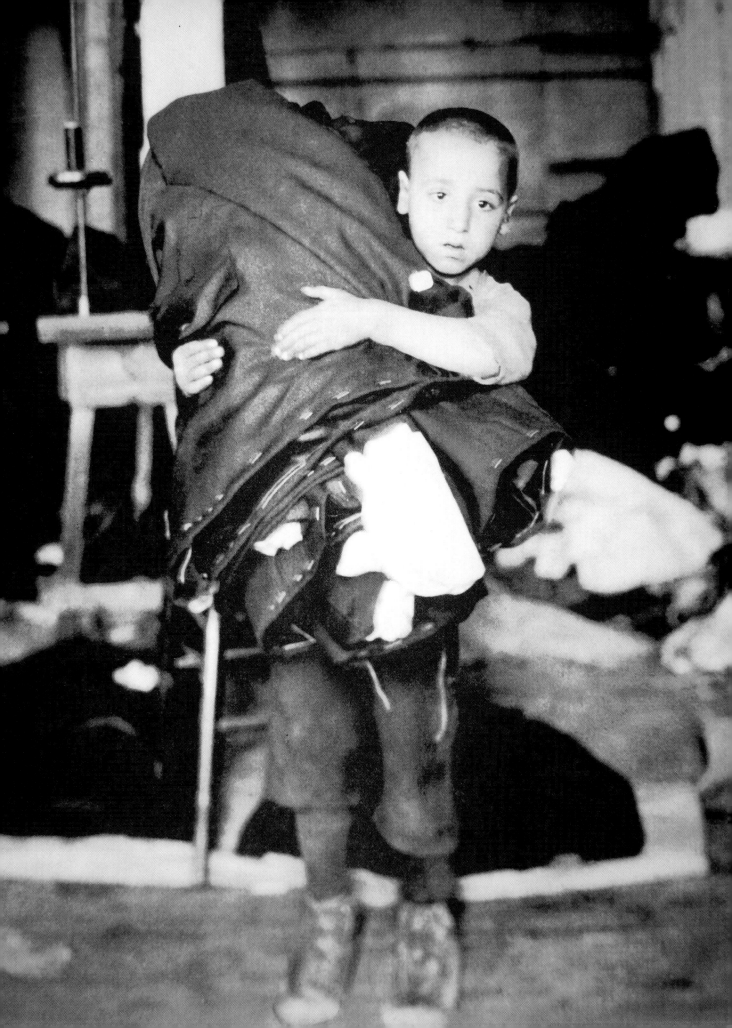

A Changing Culture

The Russian and Polish Jews who came to North America brought their traditional culture with them. They spoke a language called Yiddish and began to produce newspapers and books, poetry and plays. They changed Jewish culture in North America.

Yiddish is a mixture of Hebrew and German with some Slavic words as well. It is written in the Hebrew alphabet.

After the arrival of Russian and Polish Jews in the United States, New York City became an important Yiddish **literary** center. New Jewish newspapers, written in Yiddish, were published. The *Forward*, today published in both Yiddish and English, started as the *Jewish Daily Forward*. It was edited by a Russian-Jewish immigrant called Abraham Cahan. He wanted to help other immigrants settle into their new country. The newspaper ran a page with letters from readers asking for help and gave them answers and advice.

Many Jewish writers wrote in Yiddish about the conditions in the slums and sweatshops of New York's Lower East Side. Some wrote about life in the Pale in western Russia. Three of the most important Yiddish authors from this time are Mendele Mokher Sefarim, Isaac Leib Peretz, and Shalom Aleichem. Brothers Israel Joshua Singer and Isaac Bashevis Singer were born in Poland and immigrated to the United States. In 1978, Isaac Bashevis Singer won the Nobel Prize for Literature, one of the most important prizes for writers.

▲ Yiddish-speaking Jews from Eastern Europe kept in touch with the news through the *Jewish Daily Forward*. The paper still exists as the *Forward*.

Yiddish theater was a popular form of Jewish entertainment during the early twentieth century, especially in New York. It appealed to Jewish people of all backgrounds and from all parts of the community. The plays were comedies. They were popular because they were based on real life. They helped people to laugh at themselves and at the difficulties that they experienced in their new country.

Yiddish is no longer widely spoken in North America. However, people can learn Yiddish in some schools and colleges and can still go to Yiddish theater.

◄ **Ashkenaz: A Festival of New Yiddish Culture is an opportunity for artists to explore the Yiddish/Jewish tradition of Eastern Europe.**

Klezmer Music

Klezmer is a special kind of Jewish music. It began in Eastern Europe and Russia in the fifteenth century. Traveling musicians, called "klezmorim," played it at festivals and weddings. Klezmer music is often lively, encouraging people to dance. There are no singers, and klezmorim use instruments such as accordions, clarinets, violins, and drums. The musicians brought their instruments to North America, where klezmer music has influenced jazz and swing. Klezmer music is still popular today.

► **A modern klezmer band using a trumpet and saxophones.**

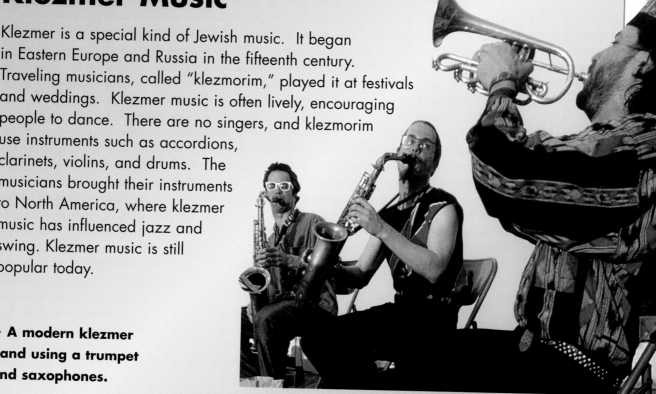

World War II (1939–1945)

The years before and during World War II were times of terror for European Jews. More than six million Jewish men, women, and children were put to death; countless others were tortured and starved.

In the 1930s, life for Jewish citizens in Germany became more and more difficult. When the Nazi Party came to power in 1933, Jews were persecuted, **assaulted**, jailed, and murdered simply for being Jewish. When Germany invaded other European countries, Jews there suffered the same horrors. The situation became even worse when, in 1942, Nazi authorities decided they wanted to **exterminate** all European Jews. Millions of Jews were rounded up and shot, or packed into freight trains and sent to concentration camps where they were murdered. This period is known as the Holocaust – Sho'ah or Hurban in Hebrew.

▲ The Nazi film *Der Ewige Jude* (*The Eternal Jew*) had a strong anti-Semitic message.

▼ Canadian fascists, who were anti-Jewish, preparing leaflets in support of the Nazis.

The Canadian Experience

In 1881 there were only 2443 Jewish people living in Canada, and most of them were in Montréal. After 1902, Jews wanting to immigrate to Canada were given help by the Jewish Colonization Association. This organization encouraged immigrants to settle in Western Canada. By 1911, the number of Jewish people throughout the country had risen to 74,564. However, when the Nazis were in power in Germany and millions of Jews were being executed, only 5000 Jews were allowed into Canada. The government and people did not want more immigrants entering the country. They turned away thousands of refugees, desperate to flee the horrors of the Holocaust.

▶ **Jews in Toronto, Canada, hold a public demonstration demanding that Nazi war criminals be put on trial.**

In North America, the attitude towards immigrants had changed. The Great Depression in the 1930s had been a time of mass unemployment. It was very hard for Americans and Canadians to find work. Most people were against letting more immigrants into the country, even when they knew about the horrors Jews faced in Nazi Germany. They thought the newcomers might take jobs away from them. In 1939, for example, the U.S. government refused to allow the 907 Jewish-German **refugees** off the SS *St. Louis*. The ship was also turned away in Canada and Cuba, and the refugees had to go back to Germany.

In spite of these difficulties, between 1931 and 1941, more than 160,000 Jews found refuge in the United States. During this time and after the war, Germany lost many of its most talented citizens, including some of its best-known authors and scientists, who fled to North America.

◀ **The SS *St. Louis* was turned away from North America.**

The Jewish Religion

Judaism is the religion of the Jewish people. Although not all Jews follow their religion, those who do, and many who do not, celebrate Jewish festivals.

◄ At his bar mitzvah, a Jewish boy is called to read the Torah in the synagogue for the first time.

For Jews, the holy day of the week is the Sabbath — *Shabbat*. It begins at sunset on Friday and ends after dark on Saturday. The start of the Sabbath is celebrated in the home with the lighting of the Sabbath candles by the woman of the household. The family shares an evening meal, which traditionally includes challah, or braided bread, which is blessed with the wine before the meal.

The Sabbath is also celebrated in the synagogue, the religious center of the Jewish community. A family may go to the synagogue to mark the Sabbath on Friday as well as on Saturday. The synagogue is a place of worship and prayer, and a center of learning, where children and adults can learn Judaism, take lessons in Hebrew, the language of the Jewish religion, and study the Torah, a set of handwritten **scrolls** containing Jewish laws, stories, and teachings.

Jewish Food

Special Jewish dishes are made for festivals. Passover food includes an unleavened bread called matzoh. Challah is a braided egg bread usually eaten on the Sabbath and other holidays. Both bagels and knish, stuffed, fried squares of dough, are available from fast-food vendors. Sweet potato kugel is a baked pudding. Jews who follow the religious teachings have strict rules about how to prepare and cook their food. Food prepared according to these laws is known as kosher.

▲ Jewish food: flat matzohs, braided challah bread, curled bagels, and triangular stuffed pastries, called borekas.

▲ A Jewish family gathers to light the Sabbath candles.

In Jewish families, boys take on religious responsibility at the age of thirteen, at their bar mitzvah. Recently, in some synagogues, girls have started to celebrate a similar ceremony, known as bat mitzvah, at the age of twelve.

There are several main festivals and many smaller ones that are celebrated each year, both at home and in the synagogue. They are a vital part of Jewish tradition, because they commemorate Jewish history. Two of the most important festivals are Passover, celebrated in the spring, and Rosh Hashanah, celebrated in the fall. During Passover, the Jewish people remember when, thousands of years ago, their ancestors escaped from slavery in Egypt. Rosh Hashanah, or Jewish New Year, is the first of ten days when Jews ask forgiveness for the mistakes they made over the past year. During the holiday, they eat apples dipped in honey to symbolize their hope that the new year will be sweet.

▶ During the festival of Hannukkah, a girl sings a song in front of a menorah, a candlestick that holds many candles. Hanukkah is an eight-day festival.

Here to Stay

Some Jews who came to North America quickly made a comfortable new life for themselves and their families. Many others, however, had to struggle against enormous odds to succeed.

J ewish immigrants from Germany were among the pioneers who went to the south and west of the United States. Many were peddlers. Through hard work, they eventually opened their own shops and were able to give their families a better life. In Canada, some Jews traveled west to farm on the prairies, or opened stores in the fast-growing cities.

Most Jews, however, stayed in the east. Life for first-generation Jews was difficult, but they dreamed of a better life for their children, many of whom followed professions in law, banking, and medicine. Some became artists in the areas of literature, music, the theater, and the entertainment industry.

▲ Habitat, an apartment block in Montréal, was designed by the Jewish architect Moshe Safdie.

▼ Stephen Spielberg on a poster with his many film titles around him.

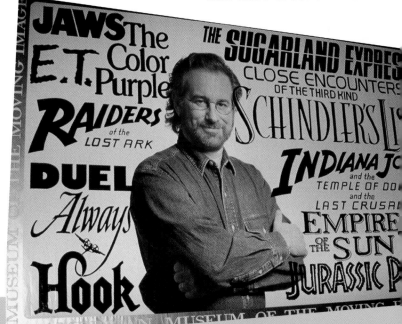

30

Mr. Music

Irving Berlin is probably America's most famous songwriter. He was born in Russia in 1888 and arrived in New York at the age of five. By the time he was in his twenties, he had written and published *Alexander's Ragtime Band*. Other Berlin songs include *Easter Parade*, *God Bless America*, and *White Christmas*. Altogether, Irving Berlin wrote the words and music to more than 800 songs.

► **Irving Berlin, whose first jobs included being a singing waiter.**

▲ **Madeleine Albright, the U.S. Secretary of State, had Jewish parents who raised her as a Catholic after escaping from Nazis in Czechoslovakia.**

In 1802, Samson Simpson was the first Jew to graduate from Columbia University and to practise law. He founded the world-renowned Mt. Sinai Hospital.

Samuel Goldwyn, the motion-picture producer, was born in Warsaw, Poland. He arrived in the United States at the age of fourteen. In 1917, he founded a film studio which later became Metro–Goldwyn–Mayer. He launched the careers of many movie stars, including the Jewish Americans Eddie Cantor and Danny Kaye. Stephen Spielberg, one of the most successful directors of all time, explored his Jewish history in the Oscar-winning movie *Schindler's List*.

Mordecai Richler, the Canadian novelist, wrote about life in the Jewish quarter of Montréal in *The Apprenticeship of Duddy Kravitz* and *Solomon Grundy Was Here*. Popular children's writer Judy Blume was brought up in New Jersey and studied at New York University. Poet, songwriter, and musician, Leonard Cohen, was born in Montréal in 1934. The Holocaust is often a theme of his work.

Jews, and the descendants of Jews, who fled their homelands to escape persecution and discrimination have found freedom and equality in North America. In return, they have made rich contributions to the cultural, economic, political, and scientific life of the United States and Canada.

Glossary

ancestry Family line going back in time.

assassinate To murder by sudden or secret attack, usually from political or religious motives.

assault Physical attack on someone.

bereaved Left sad because someone has died.

Christian A person who follows the teachings of Jesus Christ and the Bible.

colonist Someone who lives in a colony.

communal Shared by a number of people.

culture A group of people's way of life, including their language, beliefs, and art.

czar A Russian king.

descendant A family member, such as a child, grandchild, or one of their children.

destination The place that travelers are trying to get to.

discriminate To treat people unfairly because of their race, sex, or religion.

disembark To get on to land from a ship.

emigrant Someone who leaves their country to make a new life in another country.

entrepreneur Business person.

expel To order people to leave.

exterminate To kill each and every member of a whole group of people.

immigrant Someone who comes to settle in one country from another.

intolerant To be critical of the ways of another group of people.

literacy Reading and writing.

literary To do with books and reading.

massacre Mass murder.

melancholy Sad.

minority A smaller number.

Muslim A follower of Islam.

nationality The country from which a person takes a part of their identity.

peddler A person who travels about selling goods.

persecution Cruel treatment, especially in a systematic way.

profession A job that may involve a long period of study.

prosper To become successful and wealthy.

race A group of people with the same origin or skin color.

refugee Someone who has to escape from their country for fear of war and other danger.

scroll A book that is written on a long sheet of paper that is rolled around a central stick.

survivor Someone who might have died but did not.

tenement A building split into small, rented apartments.

Index

1 2 3 4 5 6 7 8 9 0 Printed in the USA 5 4 3 2 1 0